COUGARS

COUGARS

by Lynn M. Stone

A Carolrhoda Nature Watch Book

Carolrhoda Books, Inc. / Minneapolis

CONTENTS

A Cougar by Any Other Name   5
Cougar Country   12
The Hunter   15
Raising Kittens   24
Cougars and People   29
Endangered Cougars   38
Glossary   46
Index   47

Carolrhoda Books, Inc. c/o The Lerner Publishing Group
241 First Avenue North, Minneapolis, MN 55401 U.S.A.

Website address: www.lernerbooks.com

LIBRARY OF CONGRESS CATALOGING-IN-PUBLICATION DATA

Stone, Lynn M.
    Cougars / by Lynn M. Stone.
        p.   cm.
    "A Carolrhoda nature watch book."
    Includes index.
    Summary: Describes the life cycle, habits, and endangered status of the animal known as the cougar, mountain lion, puma, or panther.
    ISBN 1-57505-050-1 (alk. paper)
    1. Pumas — Juvenile literature. [1. Pumas.
2. Endangered species.] I. Title.
QL737.C23S767 1999
599.75'24 — dc21   97-16491

Manufactured in the United States of America
1 2 3 4 5 6 – JR – 04 03 02 01 00 99

A COUGAR BY ANY OTHER NAME

By whatever name you know it, the cougar (or mountain lion, puma, or panther) is the most widespread of the American wildcats. In fact, the cougar has the largest **range,** or living area, of any mammal in the entire western half of the world! These wildcats live in North, Central, and South America. Cougars in northern Canada prowl to within 500 miles (800 kilometers) south of the Arctic Circle, and South American cougars roam to the southern tip of the continent.

In Florida, cougars are called panthers.

The cougar's living area was once even greater. Because of the huge space in which it roamed, the cougar was given a variety of names by different regional groups around the United States. In much of the West, the cougar, the name by which this cat is perhaps best known, is known as the mountain lion. It is the puma in the Southwest. In Florida, it is the panther. Old Yankees in New England call it the catamount. The cat is also known by several nicknames, such as "painter," "mountain screamer," and "deer tiger."

Scientists throughout the world know the cougar by a single name—*Felis concolor*. There are differences—mostly in color and size—between groups of cougars in different regions, but these are minor.

While all cougars are basically the same, they do come from very different places and population groups. A cougar living along a steamy river in Belize is not quite the same kind of cougar you'd find perched on a cliff in Colorado. Cougars from cold places, for example, tend to be larger and have lighter-colored fur than cougars from warm places. Scientists have found that northern animals are often larger than their southern cousins. Arctic wolves are larger than Mexican wolves. The red foxes of Alaska are bigger than the red foxes of Missouri. This difference may be explained by the advantage that large size offers in keeping warm. A larger animal's body has less surface area per pound than a smaller one. That means it has less area through which to lose heat in a cold climate.

Cougars from the northwestern United States (right), *are generally larger than cougars from warmer areas, such as the Florida panther* (above).

Over many years, populations of cougars have **adapted** to their own particular surroundings. Consider Florida's panther. Its ancestors have lived in the swamps for thousands of years. These cougars have developed the ability to deal with hot, humid weather and wet paws. They probably could not deal immediately with the numbing cold that heavily furred Idaho cougars endure easily. Nor would they have—or need—the highly developed shoulder muscles and strength that make it possible for their Idaho relatives to kill elk. In turn, the Idaho cougars would find southern Florida a bit too warm and too wet for comfort.

Scientists call these far-flung groups of cougars **subspecies,** having enough minor differences for scientists to consider them a slightly different version of the same kind of animal. Some authorities recognize as many as 36 different cougar subspecies. Although the eastern cougar may be **extinct,** having no members of the subspecies still alive, the eastern cougar and the rare Florida panther both lived in the eastern half of the United States. But because of minor differences in size and color, each group is considered a subspecies.

Animals can live only within the habitats to which they have adapted. For example, a red-headed woodpecker finds food and makes shelters in trees. This bird could not survive in a cattail marsh, but it thrives in certain kinds of forest habitats. On the other hand, the long-legged, fish-eating heron would starve if it had to live in the woodpecker's forest.

The woodpecker's special bill is adapted to hammer at tree bark and then pluck insects from the wreckage. The heron's bill is adapted to spear the fish and other wriggly water creatures found in its environment. Over time, each animal has developed the means to survive in some special place, or **niche,** in the environment. What's amazing about the cougar is that over centuries it has adapted to survive in many different places—in the same way that people can survive in different places.

Depending upon the time of year and the place, cougars may prowl swamps, lowland forests, mountain forests and meadows, deserts, and grasslands. A cougar that grows up in the western mountains has no problem moving into lowland habitats if the supply of mountain food becomes scarce. The cougar is just being adaptable, changing its needs to meet the supply of food.

A hoary marmot. If the supply of deer is low, cougars can adapt by eating other mammals, such as marmots.

The Canada lynx (left) *and the bobcat* (below), *two of the cougar's North American relatives, are both smaller than the cougar.*

The cougar is easily the largest of the North American wildcats that live north of Mexico. It may top 200 pounds (90 kg) and have a body length up to 9 feet (2.7 m). Even a cougar of average size—perhaps 130 pounds (58 kg) for an adult male—dwarfs its **feline,** or cat family, cousins. The lynx is the next biggest of the cats in the United States and Canada, and it rarely weighs more than 60 pounds (27 kg). Other North American wildcats, such as the bobcat, the ocelot, the margay, and the jaguarundi, are smaller still. South of the U.S. border, however, the jaguar tops the cougar in size. The jaguar, a boxy, New World version of the leopard, may reach 300 pounds (135 kg).

No one is likely to confuse a cougar with other American wildcats. The cougar has a long, lean body and a long tail. Its head is small for such a large body. The cat's thick, short fur can be brownish, cream colored, gray, or nearly black. Some Central American cougars are brick colored. They are nicknamed "red tigers." *Felis concolor* means "cat of one color," but cougars are actually two colors—they are trimmed with white.

A cougar by any other name is still *Felis concolor,* a powerful package of fang, claw, and muscle. But the cougar doesn't strut its stuff. Normally, it's a highly secretive animal. Its lifestyle is like a hermit's, shy and solitary. Because of this, some Native American groups have given the cat the nickname "ghost walker."

COUGAR COUNTRY

Cougars don't like to share ground with other cougars or with people. They prefer wild, unsettled country. Cougars live in many kinds of places, or **habitats.** Although there are many differences between their habitats, each one must provide the cougar with food, hiding places, and a place to raise its kittens safely. All cougar habitats have another common feature—deer, a favorite and important cougar food. Deer of one kind or another live wherever cougars are found.

A white-tailed deer fawn. Cougars live in a variety of habitats, but wherever there are cougars, you can be sure there are deer, too.

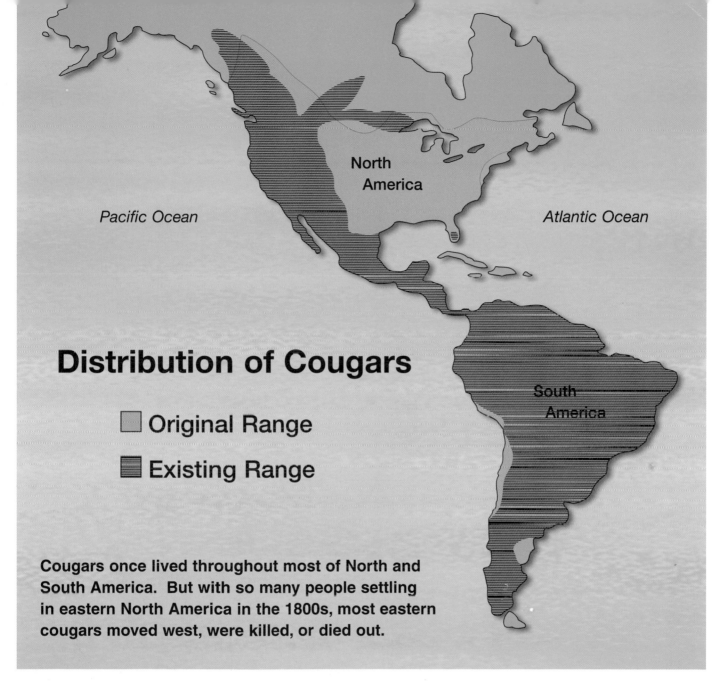

Distribution of Cougars

- ☐ Original Range
- ▤ Existing Range

North America

Pacific Ocean

Atlantic Ocean

South America

Cougars once lived throughout most of North and South America. But with so many people settling in eastern North America in the 1800s, most eastern cougars moved west, were killed, or died out.

Most cougars in North America are found in the West. Cougars once lived throughout the mainland United States. But as people changed the wilderness into villages, ranches, and roads, U.S. cougar country shrank rapidly. Settlers generally regarded cougars as nuisances and varmints. They thought cougars were dangerous to both people and livestock, animals such as cattle that are raised for food. In the East, settlers shot and killed cougars until there were almost none left to shoot.

13

But cougars found some security in the western mountain country. This is still, in large part, a rugged land of peaks, cliffs, high meadows, rushing rivers, and thick forests, where human settlements are less common than elsewhere in the country. Cougars here roam mountain ranges more than 10,000 feet (3,000 m) above sea level. No wonder American settlers in the West chose the name "mountain lion" for their big cats. In the mountains of Ecuador, cougars have climbed into mountain meadows 14,000 feet (4,200 m) above sea level. This is well above the timberline, the highest altitude at which trees can grow.

The last cougars in the East are probably those of the Florida group. Without mountains to haunt, Florida's cougars have found their niches in dark forests of pine and in swamps of bald cypress near the southern tip of the state. Rather than roaming through mountain meadows, Florida's cougars prowl humid, leafy jungles just above the sea's reach.

THE HUNTER

Each cougar hunts in its own private preserve, called a **home range.** A house cat treats its home and yard as personal property. A cougar does the same with a bigger expanse of land. Male cougars, on average, have much larger territories than females. A male cougar's home range may cover more than 300 square miles (780 km²). In cold climates, deep snow makes it harder to travel, so a cougar's territory shrinks in winter.

Adult cougars, except for females with kittens, are solitary. To help avoid contact with other adult cougars, a cougar marks the boundaries of its territory. To do this, the cat leaves scratch marks on trees and logs. It also leaves droppings and urine on little mounds of leaves and twigs. These sight and scent markers are signposts. They tell other cougars that an area is already occupied. The signs probably also give cougars other information, such as whether the territory belongs to a male or a female.

A cougar prowls its home range.

Cougars rarely fight over territory. A stray cougar can usually roam through another cat's territory without being attacked. Once a cougar knows another cougar is nearby, it seems to go out of its way to avoid a meeting. The territorial system is apparently based on mutual respect instead of on fang and claw.

Wherever it lives, the cougar is a master **predator,** or hunter. Like other meat-eating animals, this **carnivore** survives by hunting and killing. Its 30 teeth are adapted to grasp, puncture, and slice. The cougar's mouth works like a bayonet, scissors, saw, and grinder combined. Like a giant house cat returned to the wild, a cougar is driven by its instincts to stalk, attack, and kill prey. A cougar will occasionally snatch a bite or two of carrion, an animal that is long dead. But the cougar is too skillful a hunter to bother often with carrion. Every inch of a cougar's sleek, agile body is built for the chase.

Cougars are swift runners.

A cougar has exceptional spring in its hind legs. An adult cougar can leap more than 20 feet (6 m) forward from a walking pace. It can bound high into the air and still land easily and upright. When a cougar wants to be in a tree, it bounds up onto a branch. A cougar doesn't have much grace in trees, but it's nevertheless a fine climber.

The cougar is also a quick, graceful runner. It won't run fast for very long, and it will never challenge a cheetah's speed of 70 miles per hour (112 km/h). But a cougar can still run about twice as fast as any human being. The cougar's shot-from-a-gun quickness is often enough to win a short race with its prey. Unlike their cousins the jaguars and the tigers, cougars are not fond of water. They can swim if necessary, however, especially if they're being chased by dogs.

A cougar pauses to watch, listen, and sniff.

Cougars always seem to be nervously looking, listening, and sniffing. Their senses never take more than a catnap. A cougar's nose isn't as finely tuned as a wolf's or a bear's. But the cougar still has a sharp sense of smell, and its hearing is even sharper. Better still is the cougar's vision. Its eyes probably work as well as ours do in daylight, and at night, the cat's eyes work better than ours. Night vision is important for cougars because they often hunt in dim light and near darkness.

With its strength, quick reflexes, toothy jaws, and paws full of claws, a cougar is capable of killing almost any animal it finds. But big predators tend to avoid tests of strength. Large predators, such as cougars, wolves, and grizzly bears, usually stay away from each other. By doing so, they don't compete for food or risk injury by fighting over it. Cougars do sometimes attack smaller predators, including bobcats and coyotes, and kill them.

Cougars also try to avoid attacks on the biggest and healthiest **prey** animals, since those animals are harder to kill and better at defending themselves. A cougar will generally avoid risks and catch very young or very old prey if it can. But that doesn't mean a cougar won't ever kill large, strong prey animals, such as a bull elk or a bighorn ram. Never underestimate the strength of a western cougar. With their large, strong necks and shoulders, Rocky Mountain cougars can effectively kill 800-pound (360-kg) elk and drag them several yards.

A large bighorn sheep, such as this one, can be prey for a cougar.

Most of a cougar's hunting relies on stalking. Stalking—a step forward, a pause, a crouch, another step forward, all without its prey noticing—is a well-developed feline skill.

When a cougar stalks a deer, the cougar can be as motionless as a stump. It can inch forward at an extremely slow pace. Its movement gradually leads the cat closer to the deer. When the cougar senses that it is close enough, it explodes forward with frightening quickness.

When attacking a large animal, such as a deer, a cougar often leaps onto the animal's back. The cougar drives its teeth into the deer's neck, near the base of the skull. The attack may bowl over the deer and break its neck.

A Costa Rican puma stalks silently through the forest.

Bull elk (above) *are challenging targets even for a skilled hunter like the cougar.*

Hanging on to a large, terrified animal is not a carousel ride, even for a big cougar. A cougar died when the elk it was "riding" raced under a low, sharp-pointed limb. The limb speared the cougar, killing it. Another cougar, trying to wrestle a bighorn ram down, died when both the cat and the ram tumbled off a cliff. Most contests between a cougar and its prey, however, end quickly and without injury to the cat.

After a successful hunt, the cougar eats its fill, using its strong, sharp teeth to tear meat from bone. Then it covers whatever is left of the carcass (the prey animal's body) with dirt, branches, and leaves. The cougar will keep returning to the kill for several days, until the carcass has been stripped. When a carcass begins to spoil in warm weather, the cougar will leave it to creatures whose eating habits are less picky than its own.

Even though members of the deer family are a favorite prey, the cougar readily hunts other animals when deer are scarce. In various areas across North America, cougars may dine at times on mountain goat, bighorn sheep, moose, elk, wild pig, beaver, rabbit, coyote, marten, skunk, raccoon, turkey, armadillo, and porcupine. For appetizers, a cougar may eat fish, grasshoppers, and even slugs.

A cougar tears into the carcass of a mule deer.

Left: *The sharp quills of a porcupine make it difficult for a cougar to catch and kill.*
Below: *This cougar has captured a snowshoe hare.*

Catching grasshoppers and slugs does not require great skill. Even people can catch *them.* Porcupines, though, are tricky. Their bodies and tails are pincushions of sharp, barbed quills. The cougar's trick is to flip a porcupine onto its back. Since the porcupine's belly isn't protected by quills, the cougar strikes there.

A cougar kitten

RAISING KITTENS

Female cougars are ready to mate and have kittens by the time they are three years old. Nearby males find a female that is ready to mate by following her scent markings. Several males may compete for the same female. The male cougar leaves the female after mating. He has nothing to do with raising the kittens. The mother cougar considers any adult male, even the kittens' father, a threat to her babies. Any large predator, including a wolf, a grizzly, or a coyote, is a threat to kittens left untended.

The female cougar's new litter develops inside her for about three months during the **gestation** period. Before giving birth, the female finds a safe, private place to have her kittens. She may bear from one to six kittens, but three or four is an average litter.

Cougar kittens weigh about 1 pound (0.5 kg) at birth. They have spotted fur, like deer fawns, and their eyes are tightly shut. The kittens are usually born in a sheltered hollow among rocks, under roots, or among fallen branches. Until their eyes open, at about 10 days of age, they live in a world of darkness.

Cougar kittens can be born at any time of year, but most are born in late winter or early spring. They live on mother's milk entirely until they are about 6 weeks old. Then they have their first taste of meat, which their mother brings to them.

Top: *Cougar kittens have spotted fur. The spots fade gradually as the kittens grow.*
Bottom: *A mother cougar licks her kitten.*

Like young house cats, cougar kittens are playful.

By eight weeks of age, the playful kittens weigh about 10 pounds (4.5 kg). They grow rapidly on their mother's milk and on the meat she brings home. They're big enough to travel by this time. The mother leads them away from the birth site, and the kittens become little wanderers. They still stay within their mother's territory, moving from place to place as their mother searches for prey.

The first year of the little cougars' lives is in many ways the most important. That's their time with their mother, when the kittens learn how to hunt. By watching their mother, young cougars learn what to eat and how to catch it. Kittens also learn how to communicate, with hisses, growls, screams, whistlelike sounds, and chuckling. A cougar's vocabulary is much like a house cat's.

Cougars purr when they're content. Their ability to purr nonstop is one of the differences between cougars and the big cats, as scientists call lions, leopards, tigers, jaguars, and snow leopards. Cougars, too, are big, no question about that. But cougars have a voice box like that of smaller cats. The big cats have a different voice apparatus, and they have to pause for breath after a brief purr.

Hunting with their mother begins when the cougar kittens are about four or five months old. By then, the kittens weigh 25 to 35 pounds (11-16 kg). They are still playful, but they have begun to master two serious survival skills—stalking and pouncing. After another six or seven months, the kittens have lost most of the baby spots in their fur and are quickly approaching adult size.

This kitten is nearly full grown and will soon begin to hunt on its own.

Young cougars usually continue to travel and hunt with their mother until they are about two years old. But by the time they are a year and a half, young cougars have learned how to be independent. They are capable of killing prey and living alone. They may not yet sense this completely, but their mother does. She is ready to mate again and begin a new family. Eventually, she chases off her nearly grown youngsters, who move away and seek territories of their own.

Although disease and parasites kill some cougars, most of them seem to die from the effects of old age. A wild cougar that reaches the age of 12 years is considered fairly old. The animal's teeth have worn down, and its speed, strength, and agility suffer, making it less able to successfully hunt its prey. When a cougar can no longer kill, it starves to death.

COUGARS AND PEOPLE

The greatest enemies cougars have are people. The belief that cougars are dangerous to people and their livestock has been popular in North America for some four hundred years. But that view is not nearly as popular as it once was. And it is not an altogether accurate view.

Certainly, cougars are sometimes drawn to domestic animals. Corrals filled with farm animals must seem to cougars like cafeterias to kids. Serving up meals of goat, hog, horse, or cow to cougars, however, has never been part of the plan for farmers. To protect their animals, livestock owners have traditionally killed cougars. In some cases, government agencies helped ranchers destroy livestock-eating cougars with poison, traps, and professional hunters. Some of the cats were undoubtedly guilty of feeding on farm animals. Others were simply in the wrong place at the wrong time.

Cougars are hunted for sport in many parts of their range.

Large, wild cats will never be able to ignore easy prey such as farm animals. But ranchers can sometimes help avoid visits from cougars by properly housing and guarding their livestock. A large barking dog, for example, is a helpful defense against cougar attacks.

Hunters in several western states and provinces kill cougars for sport. People don't eat cougars, and cougar fur has little value, so they are not used for food or clothing. But many hunters consider cougars trophy animals because they are large, have sharp teeth and claws, and make reasonably good rugs. For some hunters, killing a cougar is considered a mark of skill.

Cougars are almost always hunted with packs of hounds. The dogs follow a cougar's scent. Eventually, the frightened cat climbs a tree to escape the yowling hounds. Once treed, the cat is an easy target for a rifle.

Cougars don't often kill full-grown, healthy deer like this one. Weak, elderly, or sickly animals are easier to catch, and by killing the weakest members of the herd, cougars help keep deer populations from becoming too large.

Over the years, some people have also hunted cougars because they believed the cats were killing too many deer and elk. Hunters preferred to have the full deer and elk herds available to themselves. Many scientists, however, have shown through field studies that cougars help weed out old, ailing, and unfit herd animals. In this way, cougars and other predators help keep the prey animals' numbers in check so that there is enough food available for all members of the herd. Without predators or hunting, deer and elk populations can grow dangerously large. Too many herd animals can destroy plant life faster than it can grow back, and eventually, the herd will face illness and starvation. It is better for the cougars, the wild herds, and human hunters if the big cats are left alive to hunt, too.

A grizzly bear with a sockeye salmon that it has caught. Like cougars, grizzlies are protected from hunting in some areas.

The easterners' war against cougars and other big predators ended long ago. Within a few generations, cougars in the East had become as rare as horsefeathers. Killing cougars was part of the process of tidying up the forest, making early America "safe" for European settlers. Many states paid hunters for killing cougars. Even at the end of the 20th century, the notion that big predators are anything except ferocious, wild-eyed beasts dies hard for some people. Texas, for example, has no closed hunting season on cougars. Texans can shoot a cougar any time of year.

In recent years, though, the attitude of most Americans toward big predators has changed. Animals such as the cougar, the wolf, and the grizzly are finding new acceptance. In national parks and other reserves (areas of land that are set aside and protected), cougars cannot be hunted. In Alaska, thousands of people visit bear reserves just to watch grizzlies catch salmon. In 1995, the United States government released wolves into Yellowstone National Park. The same government had hired professional hunters to eliminate wolves from Yellowstone in the 1920s.

The cougar has become a far greater attraction alive than dead. People generally admire the big cat, and they want it protected, at least in its wilderness retreats. California, for example, has banned cougar hunting, except in rare cases when the cats have attacked pets, farm animals, or people. And Oregon voters banned the use of dogs in hunting cougars in 1995.

Still, no one really wants to share a bike path or backyard with a cougar. There are—understandably—places where the presence of cougars won't work. Fortunately, cougars rarely choose to share space with anyone. An old Montana hunter who claimed to have killed 70 cougars said he never saw even one of the wildcats until his dogs had treed it. A cougar is usually just another ghost in the forest.

Most people would rather not run into this Florida panther or any other cougar.

Good grazing land provides food for deer, which in turn draw more cougars to an area.

Ideally, cougars would stay in the wilderness, and people in large numbers would stay out. But more and more people are moving into remote western areas—cougar hangouts. Unexpected meetings between people and cougars are becoming more common. One reason for the increase in contacts is the growing number of people. Another is the growing number of cougars, due in part to larger elk and deer herds.

Deer and elk herds are growing larger because for many years the logging industry has practiced a logging method called **clear-cutting.** When loggers clear-cut, they cut down every tree in a section of forest. This is the cheapest way to log. The results aren't pretty, but the newly cleared areas of the forest soon green up with tender new plants. These plants make terrific food for deer and elk. With a new source of food available, deer and elk numbers increase. With more plentiful prey, cougars are attracted and the cougar population grows.

Perhaps nowhere is that more true than in British Columbia. This province in western Canada has a large population of cougars. British Columbia's Vancouver Island may have more cougars per square mile than any place in North America.

In British Columbia, cougars have plenty of mountain forests and meadows, and large sections of forests have been clear-cut. Each year, more deer, more people, and more cougars call British Columbia home. Before 1994, the province had fielded only about 100 complaints a year about prowling cougars being close to houses, schools, and other buildings. The number of complaints soared to 300 in 1994. In the interest of public safety, the province had to destroy about 90 cougars. Some changes are definitely going on with cougar behavior. As time goes on, people may have to find ways to create more fear in cougars toward humans.

Haley Lake, Vancouver Island, British Columbia. The hilly, forested landscape here is ideal cougar country.

When people and cougars meet by chance, the cougar almost always flees. *Almost* always. A person who disliked house cats once said that if cats were much, much bigger, "they'd kill you!" A cougar, in many ways, seems like a huge house cat. Would it kill you?

Any wild animal, especially a big one with sharp teeth and claws, can be dangerous. No one should believe for a moment that a grizzly is somehow just a truck-sized teddy bear—or that a cougar is truly an overgrown house cat. An adult cougar certainly has the strength and weapons to kill a person. Every now and then, for reasons that aren't always clear, a cougar attacks and kills someone. A cougar that has become used to seeing people can be especially bold and dangerous. Occasionally a cougar mistakes a human jogger for prey. It may be that the person's movement triggers an attack. The cougar, in these rare cases, seems to react to a person as it might to a running deer.

Cougars may often look like large house cats, but don't be fooled. They are wild, powerful animals that should never be approached or challenged.

Fortunately, though, cougars rarely attack people. Cougar attacks killed no more than 15 people in North America during the entire 20th century. To be safe, people in cougar country can take some measures to avoid being looked upon as prey by a cougar. No one who surprises a cougar in the wild should try to approach it. Nor should that person run from the cougar. Running may increase the chances of the cougar seeing the person as prey.

ENDANGERED COUGARS

The cougar population, on the whole, has increased in recent years. Cougars have responded well to protection from hunting and to growing herds of deer and elk in many places. But no one knows just how many cougars live in North America. Being secretive and more likely to hunt by night than by day, cougars are more difficult to count than ghosts in the attic. Some biologists think that 20,000 cougars in North America is a reasonable guess. But it's strictly a guess.

The eastern cougar may still exist in small numbers somewhere in the Appalachian Mountains. Some cougars have been spotted in eastern mountain ranges. The question, though, is whether these were wild eastern cougars or simply someone's former pet. Cougars do not make good pets, especially as they grow up. But rather than find a suitable home, such as a wildlife reserve, for an unmanageable animal, people who have adopted cougar kittens from the wild sometimes release the adult cats.

The eastern cougar, then, may be **endangered**—threatened with extinction— or it may already be extinct. If it's endangered, it stands an excellent chance of becoming extinct. The cougars of Costa Rica, in Central America, also face an uncertain future. They are listed by the United States Fish and Wildlife Service as an endangered species.

Closer to home, Florida's cougars are also endangered. The state of Florida and the United States government have spent millions of dollars to help the big cats survive in Florida. Florida taxpayers have helped by purchasing special auto license plates with a picture of the Florida panther. Part of the license fee goes toward panther conservation.

In the late 1950s, when Florida's government and citizens decided to help the panther survive into the 21st century, the cat was already in trouble. Like cougars elsewhere, it had been routinely shot, trapped, and poisoned. A Florida cougar's chances of dying from old age were small indeed. The United States government finally became involved with the panther in the late 1960s. The U.S. Fish and Wildlife Service agreed with what biologists already knew—the panther had used eight of its nine lives. It was slipping rapidly toward extinction.

The U.S. Fish and Wildlife Service listed the Florida panther as an endangered species. By buying up wilderness in Florida's Big Cypress Swamp and stopping legal hunting of the panther, Florida and the United States government have managed to keep the panther from extinction. The state's panther experts say that some 30 to 50 panthers remain. Helping this tiny population rebuild its numbers is the goal of the Florida Panther Recovery Team. This team of experts has been tracking the cats with radio collars and learning about their habits—where they go, what they eat, and what they need for survival.

Florida panthers are protected in parts of the state's Big Cypress Swamp.

A panther in a Florida stream. Florida's panthers need to breed with cougars of other bloodlines if they are to survive.

One thing the team has learned is that the panther population is breeding itself out of existence. Because the population is so small, the cats are becoming too closely related. That is causing birth defects and other physical handicaps. Those problems wouldn't occur in a larger population with more bloodlines of different types.

To increase the Florida cats' chances of survival, experts have released eight female cougars from Texas in southern Florida. Biologists will study the cougars and their offspring for several years. More Texas cougars may be released in Florida someday, and the state may also be able to release some cougars that have been bred in captivity.

In Florida, the panther has become a symbol of the state's natural heritage. Schoolchildren voted it to be the state mammal. Many Floridians who will probably never see a wild panther are content just to know that the cats still live in their state.

Florida is committed to saving its panthers and their habitat, which is a wilderness of swamp and forest. There the cougars can prowl beneath the strings of Spanish moss that hang from spidery branches. Florida's cougar conservation efforts are a remarkable change of attitude for any state. After all, not long ago, most of the nation seemed bent on ridding itself of cougars entirely. People who like fur rugs haven't disappeared, but they're outnumbered by those who prefer their fur on living creatures.

A sign in southern Florida lets motorists know they are in panther country.

How many cougars we keep in North America, and where we keep them, is up to us. Cougars will always do their part. They're masters of survival. They can find a meal just about anywhere. But a cougar does need roaming room. And it needs protection from people and their activities. The cougar's future is hitched to the future of the land on which it lives. If we remain willing to set aside land for the cougar and its prey, we'll always have the company of this great, ghostly cat.

GLOSSARY

adapt: to change over time in order to survive in a specific environment

carnivore: meat-eating animal

clear-cutting: cutting down every tree in a section of a forest

endangered: at risk of losing all members of a species forever

extinct: having no members of a species still alive

feline: member of the cat family

gestation: the period of development before birth

habitat: the kind of environment in which an animal lives

home range: the area of land that one animal claims and marks as its own, where it lives, hunts, and breeds

niche: a specific place in the environment suited to a particular species

predator: an animal that hunts and kills other animals

prey: animals hunted by other animals for food

range: the geographic area in which an animal lives

subspecies: slightly different versions of an animal within a species, often living in different geographic areas

INDEX

adaptability, 9, 22, 45
adaptations, 8, 9

bighorn sheep, 19, 21, 22
bobcats, 10, 18
British Columbia, 35

Central America, 5, 11, 39
clear-cutting, 34, 35
climate, 7, 8
coloring, 7, 11, 25, 27
communication, 15, 24, 26, 27
Costa Rican cougar, 39

deer, 12, 20, 22, 31, 34, 35, 36, 38
diet, 12, 16, 22, 23, 25, 34

eastern United States, 8, 13, 14, 32, 39
elk, 19, 21, 22, 31, 34, 38
endangered status, 39, 40, 42
extinction, 8, 39, 40, 42

fighting, 16, 24
Florida, 6, 8, 14, 40, 42, 43, 44
Florida panther, 6, 8, 14, 40, 42, 43, 44

grizzly bears, 18, 24, 32, 36

habitats, 7, 8, 9, 12, 13, 14, 15, 34, 44
home range, 15
hunting behavior, 15, 16, 18–19, 20, 21, 22, 23, 26, 27, 28, 31, 38
hunting of cougars, 13, 29, 30, 31, 32, 33, 38, 40, 42, 44

jaguars, 10, 17, 27

kittens, 12, 15, 24, 25, 26, 27, 28; birth of, 25

life span, 28
livestock, 13, 29, 30

nicknames, 6, 11
North America, 5, 10, 11, 13, 29, 35, 37, 38, 45

panther. See Florida panther
population size, 34, 35, 38, 42, 43
porcupines, 22, 23
protection of cougars, 33, 40, 42, 43, 44, 45
puma, 6. See also Costa Rican cougar

raising young, 24, 26
range, 5, 6
relationship to people, 13, 29, 31, 32, 33, 34, 35, 36, 37, 40, 42, 43, 44, 45

scent marking, 15, 24
senses, 18
size, 7, 10, 11, 25
solitariness, 11, 12, 15, 16, 33, 38
sounds, 26, 27; purring, 27
South America, 5
speed, 17
stalking, 16, 20, 27
subspecies, 7, 8

teeth, 16, 20, 22, 28
territory, 15, 16, 26, 28

vision, 18

western United States, 6, 7, 8, 9, 13, 14, 19, 30, 33
wolves, 7, 18, 24, 32

ABOUT THE AUTHOR

Lynn M. Stone is an author and photographer who has written more than 250 books for young readers about wildlife and natural history, including Carolrhoda's Nature Watch titles *Vultures* and *Grizzlies,* as well as a number of titles in Lerner Publications' Early Bird Nature Books series. In addition to photographing wildlife, Mr. Stone enjoys fishing and traveling. A former teacher, he lives with his wife and daughter in Batavia, Illinois.